A Fly on the Wall Street

Learning About the Stock Market

A Fly on the Wall Street

Learning About the Stock Market

By Sandi Nelson

Illustrated by
Jared Beckstrand

Two Harbors Press
212 3rd Avenue North, Suite 290
Minneapolis, MN 55401
612.455.2293
www.TwoHarborsPress.com

ISBN-13: 978-1-938690-29-7
LCCN: 2012949593
Distributed by Itasca Books

Illustrated by Jared Beckstrand
Cover Design and Typeset by James Arneson

Printed in the United States of America

For my husband, Rick,
who has served his clients with dedication
and integrity for more than thirty years.

Hi there!
Frederick Flyberg
is my name.

I was once an ordinary housefly, until the day I landed on the wall of my pal, Leonard. Leonard was sad because some of the kids at school were bullying him, and he felt like he didn't have any friends. Leonard looked up at me and said, "Hello, my BFF." *What did that mean?* I wondered. *Hello, my **B**rilliant **F**rederick **F**lyberg?*

Leonard was actually telling me that I was his "**B**est **F**riend **F**orever." After that, Leonard and I became inseparable.

Every summer, I watched from high upon the Main Street sign as Leonard made and sold the best snow cones in the whole world!

Leonard wanted to make some money and save it so that he could buy a car one day, go to college, and in time, get a good job.

Leonard's grandfather wanted his grandson to succeed. He gave Leonard advice about what to do with the money he earned from selling snow cones. Grandpa suggested that Leonard **invest** his money. In other words, Grandpa suggested that Leonard do something with the money so that he could make even *more* money, instead of just keeping it in his piggy bank.

"Grandpas always know everything!"

Leonard was confident that by taking grandpa's advice and investing his money, he could achieve his goals.

Leonard's grandfather was right!

After he invested his money, and when Leonard was old enough, he was able to buy a car!

By investing his money, Leonard was also able to make enough money to go to college. (I went to college with Leonard, of course!)

Goals having to do with money are called **_financial goals._**

Leonard's goal of having enough money to buy a car was a financial goal. His goal of having enough money to go to college was also a financial goal.

What are some other financial goals? A goal to buy a new game system is a financial goal, because money is needed to buy that game system. You may be ambitious and want to pay to take your family on a surprise vacation. (Now that would be a *big* financial goal!) Of course, deciding to *save* and not spend any of your money is always a financial goal.

Leonard has grown up now, and he has reached another one of his goals. Today, he has a very exciting and important job in a place known as "Lower Manhattan," which is located in New York City. Now when Leonard goes to work, I sit high upon the sign that says "Wall Street."

Today, Leonard helps other people by giving *them* advice about what to do with *their* money so that they can achieve *their* goals.

Mr. Seymour Green is one of the people Leonard helps today. Mr. Green is Leonard's customer, or *client*. Leonard is Mr. Green's *financial advisor*. Leonard and Mr. Green have also become very good friends.

Mr. Green asks Leonard to suggest ways that he can invest his money. He would like to own a company, or a *corporation*. Mr. Green can't afford to buy a whole company, but Leonard suggests to him that he purchase a *part* of a company.

That's right—Leonard can help his client become a part-owner of a whole corporation! Mr. Green will have to buy *stock* in that company, and the parts of the company he can buy are called *shares* of stock. Mr. Green will become a *shareholder*. A financial advisor, like Leonard, who helps his or her clients buy shares of stock is sometimes called a *stockbroker*. Stockbrokers work in places known as *brokerage houses*.

"Wow, that will cost a lot!"

"I would like to buy a company."

Leonard remembers that when he was a child, his grandfather suggested he buy shares in a restaurant that sold fast food, because Leonard loved to eat chicken nuggets. Leonard took Grandpa's advice, and he was proud to be able to say that he was a shareholder and part-owner of a restaurant.

Do you have a favorite company? If you enjoy drinking soda pop, you might think about becoming a part-owner of a soft drink company. If you like to go to the movies, perhaps you would like to purchase stock in a motion picture company.

The shares of some of the largest and strongest companies are called **blue chip stocks**. Of course, the stocks are not actually blue, and they are not the kind of chips that you eat. Over a hundred years ago, the best stocks were given the name "blue chip" because the most valuable chips (the little round discs) used in a card game named "poker" were the blue ones!

Can't decide which company to buy stock in? You may think about buying a **mutual fund**, where an investor can own stock in many companies at once!

Companies that offer stock are represented by abbreviations, or *symbols*. You may recognize some of these companies:

McDonald's **MCD**	Toys "R" Us **TOY**
Walmart **WMT**	Apple **AAPL**
Coca-Cola **KO**	Papa John's **PIZZ**
Facebook **FB**	PetSmart **PETM**
Google **GOOG**	Walt Disney **DIS**

When you buy stock, you become a part-owner and an *investor* in that particular company. If the company makes money, or is *profitable*, the value of the stock can *rise*, or become more valuable. You can then choose to sell the stock for more than what you paid for it, or you can keep, or *hold on to* the stock and trust that the company will continue to be profitable.

Leonard first became an investor in a fast food restaurant when he took some of his earnings from his snow cone business and bought three shares of the restaurant company's stock. He paid $10 for the three shares, which means he paid about $3.33 for each share. He still had the $10 in value, but his money was now in *stock* instead of cash.

Whenever he ate chicken nuggets, Leonard thought of all the new fast food restaurants throughout the world and how many other people must also be eating chicken nuggets. Leonard believed that the fast food company must be making money, or was being profitable.

He was right! In several months, the price of Leonard's stock rose—or increased in value—to $4 a share. Even though Leonard paid $10 for the three shares, they were now worth a total of $12.

3 shares of stock worth $4 each = $12 in total

"You may have to read this a few times ... it made my head spin at first!"

If Leonard wanted to sell all of his stock, he would have earned $2 in profit. But Leonard decided to sell just *some* of his stock, so he sold one of the shares worth $4.

3 shares of stock (together) worth $12 – 1 share of stock worth $4 = $8 worth of stock, or 2 shares left.

After selling the share, Leonard still had $12, but $8 of his money was in stock, and $4 of his money was in cash.

With the $4 cash he received when he sold the one share of stock, Leonard bought more supplies for his snow cone business. He sold so many more snow cones that he made another $10 profit in cash! Leonard was happy, because he now had $18.

2 shares of stock (together) worth $8 +$10 cash = $18 in total.

But Leonard actually had more money than that, because while he was working at his snow cone stand, the 2 shares of restaurant stock that he did *not* sell, which were worth $4 each, increased in value again and rose to be worth $5 a share. His 2 shares of stock were now worth $10 in total. So, in fact, Leonard had $20!

2 shares of stock (together) worth $10 + $10 cash = $20 in total.

This time, instead of buying more supplies for his snow cone business with his cash, Leonard decided to take the $10 and buy 2 *more* shares of the restaurant stock, which remember, was now worth $5 a share. Leonard still had $20, but all of the money was now in stock.

4 shares of stock each worth $5 = $20 in total

So let's think about this: Leonard started out with 3 shares of fast food restaurant stock that he bought for $10, and in less than a year he had 4 shares of the restaurant stock worth a total of $20!

Leonard doubled his money!

But wait! There's more:

When companies are profitable, they sometimes pay **dividends** on each share of stock that an investor owns. The dividend is usually a small cash payment made to a shareholder each **quarter** of the year (every three months,) but the dividend can also be paid in extra shares of stock.

Of course, Leonard's grandfather gave him pretty good advice to buy the restaurant stock when he did. A company's stock doesn't always rise so quickly, and sometimes it doesn't rise at all. Unfortunately, stock of a company can even go *down* in value. Luckily, that didn't happen to Leonard's stock.

Buying and selling stocks is sometimes referred to as **trading stocks**. The places where shares of company stock are traded are called **exchanges**. The **New York Stock exchange**, or "**NYSE**" is one of the largest and busiest exchanges in the world.

"Ouch! That bell rings every morning at 9:30 on the East Coast when the **NYSE** opens and again at 4:00 in the afternoon when it closes."

The **National Association of Security Dealers Automated Quotations** is another exchange, but all of the stocks on this exchange are bought and sold through a computer network. Thank goodness the exchange is known just as the **NASDAQ!**

To tell the difference between stocks traded on the NYSE and stocks on the NASDAQ, you usually just need to look at the symbol. Most stocks traded on the NYSE have one to three letters, and most stocks traded on the NASDAQ have at least four or five letters. For example, McDonald's stock, or "MCD," is bought and sold on the NYSE, and PetSmart stock, or "PETM," is bought and sold on the NASDAQ. One exception to the rule is Facebook, which trades under the symbol "FB" on the NASDAQ.

When people hear the term "Wall Street," they often think about a great big **stock market**, which includes the NYSE, NASDAQ and some other exchanges, banks, and brokerage houses. Basically, anywhere investment business takes place can be referred to as **Wall Street**, even if it is not located in Lower Manhattan in New York City.

Do you have a bank in your town? If so, then that bank is part of Wall Street!

If you decide to buy stock in a company, how will you know if your investment is becoming more valuable?

If you bought stock with the help of a financial advisor, he or she will be happy to give you current information on the value of your investment. You can also get the price of stocks, or **stock quotes**, from a newspaper or from a TV business channel, and you can always look on the Internet to find the price of your stock.

Stock prices are often displayed on charts and graphs. And, at times, you may find the price of your stock scrolling or flashing across the bottom of your TV or computer screen on what is called a **ticker**. Stock symbols are often called **ticker symbols**.

"Are you wondering where the term 'ticker' came from? In the old days, stock prices were printed on ticker tape machines that went Tick ... Tick ... Tick ..."

"The Dow is up!" "The Dow is down!" Have you ever heard this before? The **Dow**, or "**DJIA**" is short for **Dow Jones Industrial Average**. But don't let that name scare you. The Dow is nothing more than a list, or **index,** of thirty "blue chip" stocks from American companies. When the Dow is "up," that just means that the value, or price, of the 30 stocks on the list—added all together—is more than it was before. When the Dow is "down," that means that the value, or price, of the 30 stocks added together is less that it was. One minute the Dow can be up, and the next minute it can be down.

When the Dow goes up, sometimes people call it a **rally**.

By the way . . . the Dow Jones Index was created way back in 1886 by a man named Charles Dow. A few years earlier, he and his friend, Edward Jones, came up with the idea of printing a bulletin that provided financial news. Of course, over one hundred years ago there were no computers, no televisions, and not even radios or cell phones, so their bulletin was very important. Charles Dow and Edward Jones named the bulletin **The Wall Street Journal**, and today it is still one of the major financial newspapers in the world!

The Dow Jones is not the only index in the world. There are many lists where stocks are grouped together. You may have heard of the **Standard and Poor's 500**, or **S&P 500**. You guessed it—there are 500 stocks in that index! The S&P 500 index includes all of the stocks on the Dow, plus 470 more. (Remember, the Dow has 30 stocks.) All of the stocks on the S&P 500 are traded on either the NYSE or on the NASDAQ.

Here are the names of some of the other indexes in the world:

FTSE 100 (100 companies in England)

HANG SENG (48 companies in China)

NIKKEI 225 (225 companies in Japan)

MICEX 10 (10 companies in Russia)

BSE SENSEX (30 companies in India)

DAX (30 companies in Germany)

IBEX 35 (35 companies in Spain)

CAC 40 (40 companies in France)

MEXBOL (33 companies in Mexico)

"You can buy parts of companies all over the world!"

Now on to my very favorite stock market terms: the **_bull market_** and the **_bear market_**.

"Bulls and bears ... my kind of stock! ... but all I've seen is that bronze statue ..."

Remember, when we hear "The Dow is up!" or "The Dow is down!" it means stocks are going up or down in value on a minute-by-minute chart.

A **bull market** is when the price or value of stocks moves **up** over a period of time.

A **bear market** is when the price or value of stocks moves **down** over a period of time.

"How's the Dow now, brown cow?"

Bull markets and bear markets that move in one direction over time can last for months, or even years.

A very famous statue of a bull is located in Manhattan, New York. The statue represents a bull market, of course.

Now you know more about Wall Street than many adults know! Understanding the stock market is not always easy, but learning about investing can be fun and exciting.

Someday you may want to become an investor in stock and be a part-owner of a corporation. Remember, having financial goals is important. Whether you hope to have enough money to buy a car or go to college, or you dream about just having a lot of money so that you can help other people, wise investing will help you to reach your goals.

You may even want to think about becoming a financial advisor yourself, so that you can assist other people when they want to invest their money.

"Hey Lenny - how about we go find a fat cat?"

"Ahh, don't be such a wise fly..."

Good luck with your future financial goals and dreams!